EAT WITH LOVE

Samira El Khafir

NEW
HOLLAND

EAT WITH LOVE

Samira El Khafir

CONTENTS

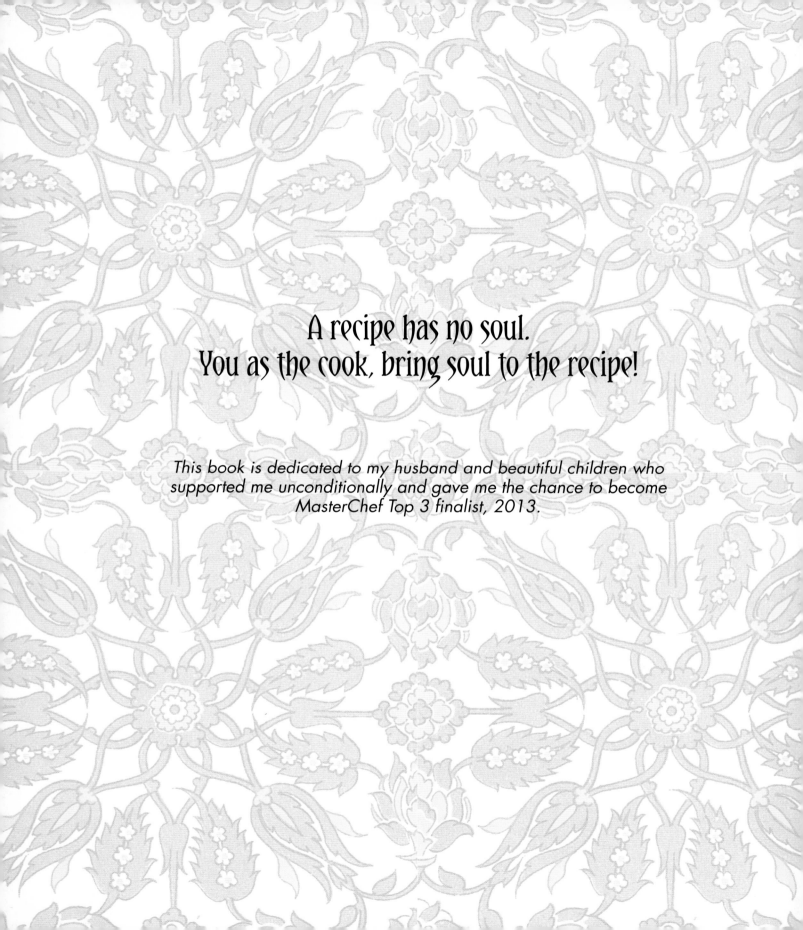

A recipe has no soul.
You as the cook, bring soul to the recipe!

This book is dedicated to my husband and beautiful children who supported me unconditionally and gave me the chance to become MasterChef Top 3 finalist, 2013.

A few words from Samira

Here I bring you my modern Middle Eastern cookbook, hoping to spread my love of Middle Eastern food to the world of food lovers.

I am the youngest of eight children (five brothers and two sisters). As we grew up, everybody knew mum's rule: no going into the kitchen. It was her domain! However, as the last sibling, I managed to break this rule when I was in my teens. My mother was unwell and needed help in the kitchen and that's where my passion for food began.

My mother makes the tastiest dishes. I have never had a meal from a chef who cooks as well as my mother. My first memory of my mother's cooking was when she would make her beautiful Lebanese sweets—I would come home from school and the whole house would smell like rose water and orange blossom.

My parents migrated from Lebanon in the late 1960s, hence my Lebanese–Australian upbringing. My parents opened their first bakery Damascus Sweets in 1976. It was an authentic Middle Eastern sweet shop. Due to personal reasons, my parents sold their business. However, this didn't stop my mother and father making their own traditional sweets and food at home. I count myself lucky to have learned how to cook authentic Lebanese foods and desserts. During my mid-20s I married an amazing man from Egypt and this is where my search for African flavours came to life.

My family has grown to be very multicultural with family from Europe, Africa, Australia and the Middle East and I am so pleased to be a part of the mixed range of nationalities in my family because it has introduced me to all different types of cuisines.

Once I joined MasterChef, season 5, I learnt so much more than I ever knew. It opened my eyes to culinary techniques and an understanding as to why I cook the way I do. I took the risk and ventured out and have produced my very own modern Middle Eastern cuisine. I have infused different flavours and techniques to what I would usually cook and turned my dishes into MasterChef quality dishes.

In this cookbook I have shared some traditional dishes and also have many of my MasterChef creations that I really hope you all enjoy.

Remember cook with love, so you can eat with love.

Samira El Khafir

Spice Mix

باهنا ولاسفا
أنءَيْ جَاكَة بَ جَ جَاكِ غَيْ خَ إَيْ إِنَّ

Lebanese spice mix

I use this in 90 per cent of the dishes I make. I hardly ever season with just cracked black pepper. This spice blend is what I have grown up with and I use it in all my food.

· ·

3½ oz/100 g whole black
   peppercorns
1¾ oz/50 g whole cloves
1¾ oz/50 g cinnamon quill
1¾ oz/50 g whole nutmeg
¾ oz/25 g cumin seeds

Makes 9½ oz/275 g

Add all the ingredients to a spice grinder or mortar and pestle and grind the spices together. Store in an airtight container.

Harissa paste

I love harissa paste as a dip or to marinate spatchcock or chicken. I find it is a little too hot for children, but for adults, it tastes amazing. You could also mix in 3 tablespoons Greek yoghurt and have it as a dip for corn chips or drizzle on top of roasted vegetables.

6 long fresh hot red chillies
3 cloves garlic, crushed
1 teaspoon salt
2 teaspoons ground cumin
2 teaspoons ground coriander
2 tablespoons olive oil

Makes enough for 1 use

Combine all the ingredients in a mortar and pestle and pound to a fine paste.

Spice rub for fish

1 tablespoon cumin seeds
1 tablespoon coriander seeds
1 tablespoon ground ginger

Makes enough for 1 large fish

Blend all the spices in a spice blender. Rub the spice mix over the fish and leave to marinate in the fridge for a few hours or overnight.

Bell pepper marinade for chicken

3 red bell peppers/capsicums
2 tablespoons ground cumin
2 bird's eye chilli
2 teaspoons salt
¼ cup olive oil

Makes enough for 1 use

Char the skin off the bell peppers by heating them over an open flame or a gas cook top. Carefully remove the peppers from the flame and place them in a plastic zip-lock bag. Leave for a few minutes. Remove the peppers and the skin should peel off easily.

Place the peeled peppers into a blender with the cumin, chilli and salt and blend well.

While the blender is on, slowly pour the oil in a steady stream until everything is combined. Cover the chicken with this mixture and leave to marinate in the fridge for at least 30 minutes—the longer the better.

You can then barbecue the chicken or grill it in the oven.

Baharat spice mix

The well-known baharat seven-spice mix tastes amazing with everything. Sprinkle on scrambled eggs, add to your lamb and beef dishes or add to your soup. Be careful not to use too much though as it is very strong. Just a little sprinkle goes a long way. I love this mix in my beef burgers and kofta—yum yum.

2 tablespoons paprika
4 tablespoons pepper
3 tablespoons cumin
2 tablespoons cinnamon
1 teaspoon cloves
1 teaspoon cardamom
1 teaspoon nutmeg

Makes 15 servings

Mix all the spices together in a bowl and store in an airtight container.

Ras el hanout

I use this mixture for tagines. And it is also great with fish or vegetarian dishes.

2 teaspoons ground ginger
2 teaspoons ground cardamom
2 teaspoons ground mace
1 teaspoon cinnamon
1 teaspoon ground allspice
1 teaspoon ground coriander seeds
1 teaspoon ground nutmeg
1 teaspoon turmeric
½ teaspoon ground black pepper
½ teaspoon ground white pepper
½ teaspoon ground cayenne pepper
½ teaspoon ground anise seeds
¼ teaspoon ground cloves

Makes 15 servings

Mix all the ingredients together in a bowl and then store in an airtight container.

Za'atar spice mix

¼ cup toasted sesame seeds
¼ cup sumac
¼ cup dried thyme leaves

Makes 1 cup

Combine the ingredients together in a bowl and store in an airtight jar.

Mezze

باهنا ولا لسفا

Za'atar scroll

1 cup za'atar mix (see recipe
    p. 23 or can be bought at
    Middle Eastern grocers)
2 cups olive oil
2½ cups all-purpose/plain flour
1 tablespoon dried yeast
3 tablespoons sugar
1 teaspoon salt
½ teaspoon baking powder
¼ cup corn oil
½ cup warm water
½ cup Greek yoghurt

Makes 20

In a small bowl, mix the za'atar mix and 1 cup of olive oil together
and set aside.

For the dough, place the dried ingredients in a bowl and give it a mix.

Create a well in the centre of the flour and add in the corn oil, yoghurt
and water. Slowly incorporate the wet ingredients into the dry. Mix well
then place on the bench and knead the dough for 10 minutes until it is
smooth and soft. If more liquid is needed, add 1 tablespoon of warm
water at a time.

Once you have kneaded the dough, drizzle a little extra corn oil and
rub it on the dough. Place the dough in a bowl, cover with a tea towel and
allow it to stand for 45 minutes.

Knock back the dough and leave for another 30 minutes.

Preheat the oven to 350°F/180°C fan-forced

Once your dough is ready, portion it into 5 balls and cover them with a
tea towel.

Roll out one of the balls of dough into a square shape $1/5$ in (½ cm) thin.
Spread out the za'atar mix all over the dough—be generous. Starting from
one edge, roll up the dough into a log shape.

Once it is into a log shape, cut through the log at ½ in (1½ cm) intervals.

Spray a muffin tin with oil and place the log slices into the muffin tin, cut
side up. Bake in the oven for 15–20 minutes until golden all over. Repeat
with the remaining balls.

Remove the pastry swirls from the tin, place onto a cooling rack and
leave to cool before serving.

Baalbakiya

Lamb mince and pine nut pastry

DOUGH

2½ cups all-purpose/plain flour
1 tablespoon dried yeast
1 teaspoon salt
1 teaspoon sugar
¼ cup olive oil
1 cup warm water

FILLING

1 onion
1 bird's eye chilli
2 tomatoes
1 lb/500 g lamb mince
salt, to taste
pinch of Lebanese spice mix (see
    recipe p. 13 or can be bought
    from Middle Eastern grocers)
¼ cup pine nuts, toasted

Makes 20

To make the dough, place all the dried ingredients in a large bowl and mix to combine. Make a well in the centre of the flour and add in the wet ingredients. Mix well then turn out onto a floured bench top and knead for 10 minutes until the dough is soft to the touch.

Place the dough in a bowl, rub with oil, cover with a tea towel and set aside in a warm area for at least 40 minutes.

Knock back the pastry and leave to rest for another 20 minutes.

Preheat the oven to 350°F/180°C fan-forced. Line a baking tray with baking paper.

For the filling, place the onion, chilli and tomato in a blender for 30 seconds. Add the minced meat and blend for a further 30 seconds

Place the meat mixture in a bowl and add the seasoning and pine nuts. Stir to combine.

Portion the dough into 3 balls and cover with a tea towel.

Roll out one of the dough balls to 4 mm thin then cut out circles using a 2 in (1 cm) pastry cutter.

Place a tablespoon of mixture on top of each circle. Bring each corner into the middle of the circle, over the meat, to make a square shape. Pinch the edges together. Repeat with the remaining dough and filling.

Place the square pastries onto a lined tray and bake in the oven for 20 minutes or until golden on the edges.

Note: The baalbakiya can be frozen once cooked, just defrost and place in the oven at 350°F/180°C fan-forced for 10 minutes to heat through.

Tabouli

3 tomatoes, finely diced
1 cucumber, peeled and finely diced
2 scallions/spring onions, finely
   sliced
heart of an iceberg lettuce, finely
   shredded
1 large bunch parsley, finely
   shredded stalks and leaves
¼ cup fine bulgur
salt, to taste
juice of 2 lemons
¼ cup olive oil

Serves 4

In a large bowl, add the tomato, cucumber, scallions, lettuce and parsley then sprinkle the bulgur and salt on top. Set aside and leave until ready to serve.

About 5 minutes before serving, add the lemon juice and olive oil and toss lightly until all combined. Taste to adjust the salt—the tabbouli should be full of flavour and a little tangy.

Fried eggplant salad

corn oil, for deep-frying

1 pita bread, cut into little squares

1 eggplant, diced

1 iceberg lettuce, finely sliced

1 small Spanish onion, finely sliced

2 cucumbers, finely sliced

1½ cup chickpeas

1 x 150 g/5 oz corn, drained

SAUCE

½ cup Greek yoghurt

½ cup mayonnaise

1 clove garlic, crushed

1 chilli, finely chopped

salt, to taste

pepper, to taste

3 teaspoons lemon juice

Serves 4

In a deep-fryer, heat up corn oil to a temperature of 350°F/180°C. If you don't have a deep fryer, heat the oil in a deep frying pan over a high heat. To test if the oil is hot enough, drop a piece of bread in the oil. If it browns within 30 seconds, the oil is ready. Fry the bread until golden. Remove and drain on paper towel.

Fry the eggplant until golden. Remove and drain on paper towel. Season with salt.

On a large platter, arrange the lettuce, onion, cucumber, corn, fried bread, eggplant and lastly the chickpeas in layers, one on top of the other.

In a separate bowl, mix the sauce ingredients all together.

Drizzle the salad dressing over the top of the salad just before serving.

Dukkah asparagus with Greek yoghurt

DUKKAH
½ cup hazelnuts
1 tablespoon cumin seeds
1 tablespoon coriander seeds
2 tablespoons pine nuts
1 tablespoon sesame seeds
1 teaspoon salt

1 tablespoon olive oil
1 bunch asparagus
1 tablespoon Greek yoghurt

Serves 2

Preheat the oven to 350°F/180°C.

To make dukkah, place hazelnuts on a tray and place in the oven to toast for 10 minutes.

Take hazelnuts out and place them on a tea towel while still hot. Rub the tea towel with the hazelnuts inside. This will remove most of the skin from the hazelnuts.

Place the cumin seeds and coriander seeds in a small pan over a medium heat and toast for 30 seconds. Pour the toasted spices, the hazelnuts, pine nuts, sesame seeds and salt in a blender and blend for 30 seconds. Leave the dukkah mixture a little coarse if you prefer.

In a medium pan, heat the olive oil over a medium heat. Once pan is hot, cook the asparagus and turn them after 30 seconds. I personally do not like my asparagus over-cooked, I like it still crisp.

Place the asparagus on a plate with a dollop of yoghurt and a sprinkle of the dukkah.

Cheese and vegetable pastry

DOUGH

2½ cups all-purpose/plain flour

1 tablespoon dried yeast

1 teaspoon salt

1 teaspoon sugar

¼ cup olive oil

1 cup warm water

FILLING

1 cup feta cheese, finely diced

½ cup mushroom, finely sliced

½ cup Spanish olives, sliced

½ cup tomato, finely diced

1 teaspoon thyme leaves, chopped

1 teaspoon oregano leaves, chopped

Makes 20

To make the dough, place all the dried ingredients in a large bowl and mix to combine. Make a well in the centre of the flour and add in the wet ingredients. Mix well then turn out onto a floured benchtop and knead the dough for 10 minutes until soft to the touch.

Place the dough in a bowl, rub with oil, cover with a tea towel and set aside in a warm area for at least 40 minutes.

Knock back the pastry and leave to rest another 20 minutes.

Preheat the oven to 350°F/180°C fan-forced. Line a baking tray with baking paper.

For the filling, place all ingredients in a bowl and give everything a quick toss.

Portion the dough into 2 balls and cover with a tea towel.

Roll out one of the balls of dough to 4 mm thin and cut using a circle pastry cutter to desired size.

Place 1 tablespoon of mixture in centre of the circle fold the pastry over and pinch the pastry together to form a moon shape.

Spray the pastry with oil and place on the lined tray. Bake in the oven for 20 minutes or until golden.

Shaklish with tomato and onion

1 shaklish (aged set yoghurt with
  spices, can be bought at Middle
  Eastern grocers)
½ small onion, finely diced
1 tomato, finely diced
2 tablespoons olive oil

Serves 4

Wash the herbs off the shanklish. Pat dry and crumble into a bowl.
  Add the onion, tomato and olive oil. Give everything a toss.
  Delicious on top of salads or eaten with pita bread as part of a mezze.

Cucumber and tomato salsa

1 cucumber, finely diced
1 tomato, finely diced
4 basil leaves, finely sliced
2 tablespoons olive oil
salt, to taste

Serves 2

Place all ingredients in a bowl and season with salt to taste. Stir until
combined.
  Serve this as part of a mezze platter or as a side dish.

Homemade flat bread

2½ cups all-purpose/plain flour
1 tablespoon dried yeast
½ teaspoon salt
½ teaspoon sugar
1½ cups warm water
a drizzle of olive oil (or 1 tablespoon
   melted unsalted butter)

Makes 30

To make the dough, place all the dried ingredients in a large bowl and mix to combine. Make a well in the centre of the flour and add in the wet ingredients, except the oil. Mix well then turn out onto a floured bench top and knead the dough for 10 minutes until soft to the touch.

Place the dough in a bowl, cover with a tea towel and set aside in a warm area for at least 40 minutes.

Knock back the pastry and leave to rest for another 30 minutes.

Portion the dough out into about 30 medium-sized balls and place a tea towel over the dough so it does not dry out.

Place a non-stick pan on the stove over a medium heat and wait until it starts to smoke—be careful this will be very hot.

While you are waiting for the pan to come up to heat, roll out one of the dough balls very thinly into a round shape not larger than the pan.

Place in the hot pan for 30 seconds then turn over. You will notice the bread will start to bubble and make air pockets—this is what you are hoping to achieve. Once golden on both sides, take the bread off and place the cooked bread to rest on a tea towel. Repeat with the remaining balls of dough.

If you'd like to add some flavour to your flatbread, once the bread is off the stove, rub the hot bread with a knob of unsalted butter.

Tesiya

Crisp bread with chickpeas, yoghurt and tahini sauce with pine nuts

2 x 9 oz/250 g cans chickpeas
Lebanese spice mix (see recipe
    p. 13 or purchased from Middle
    Eastern grocers)
4 tablespoons ghee (clarified butter)
1 pita bread, torn up into bite-sized
    pieces, fried or grilled
3 tablespoons tahini paste
juice of 1 lemon
36 oz/1 kg Greek yoghurt
2 tablespoons pine nuts

Serves 4

Drain and rinse the chickpeas and place into a pot. Just cover them with water, season with salt to taste and add ½ teaspoon Lebanese spice mix. Bring the chickpeas to a boil, then lower the heat and simmer until very tender, about 5 to 10 minutes.

In the meantime, heat a pan over a high heat. Add 2 tablespoons of ghee and, once melted, add your bread and toss until the ghee is absorbed and the bread turns golden. Pour the bread onto a serving tray and allow to cool.

In a bowl, whisk together the tahini paste and lemon juice until it thickens. Add the yoghurt and continue to whisk until it is all combined. Season with salt to taste.

In the same pan you toasted the bread, heat the rest of the ghee over a medium heat. Once melted, toast the pine nuts and stir until they turn light gold. Pine nuts will burn easily if left unattended so keep an eye on them.

Strain the chickpeas, reserving the liquid.

To assemble, in a bowl, lightly mash up half of the chickpeas with a fork and then add the other half and stir. Add a tablespoon at a time of the chickpea liquid on top of the chickpeas and stir until it becomes into a looser mixture. Season to taste with salt and a pinch of Lebanese spice mix.

Pour the chickpeas on top of the bread and pour 3 tablespoons of liquid on top so it does not dry out. Drizzle over the tahini yoghurt and then sprinkle with the toasted pine nuts and any leftover ghee from the pan.

Shakshouka

This is a dish of eggs poached in a delicious tomato sauce, similar to the Israeli shakshuka. Serve this as part of a hearty breakfast with a side of fresh pita bread and hummus.

1 tablespoon ghee (clarified butter you can use olive oil for a healthier option)
1 onion, finely diced
1 clove garlic, crushed
3 tomatoes, peeled and finely diced
salt, to taste
pinch of ground cumin
4 eggs
pinch of cracked pepper
1 tablespoon parsley, finely shredded

Serves 4

Place a medium-sized pan on the stove on medium heat. Add the ghee to the pan and, once it has melted, add the onion and garlic and cook, stirring constantly for 2 minutes, until the onion becomes tender and does not colour.

Add the tomato and stir until it breaks down. Season with salt and cumin.

Crack the 4 eggs on top of the tomato, evenly around the pan.

Lower the heat and cook for 2 minutes so the yolk is still runny.

Season with salt and cracked pepper and sprinkle with parsley. Take the pan straight to the table to serve.

Labneh

Set yoghurt

2 lb 3 oz/1 kg unsweetened Greek
  yoghurt
good pinch of salt

Makes 1 kg labneh

Place the yoghurt into a bowl. Add the salt and mix well.

Line a sieve with a clean dish cloth or muslin and place the sieve over a bowl. Pour the yoghurt into the lined sieve.

Place the bowl in the fridge overnight to drain. The next day, place the drained labneh in a sterilised container and store in the fridge.

Note: This is a basic labneh recipe, which can be eaten with preserved olives and pita bread.

Spiced labneh

1 quantity labneh (see recipe above)
pinch of cayenne pepper
zest of 1 lemon
1 tablespoon thyme leaves, finely
  chopped
olive oil

Makes 15 balls

Make your basic labneh recipe but leave the yoghurt to set for 48 hours.

Place the labneh in a bowl and season with cayenne pepper, lemon zest and finely chopped thyme leaves. Mix well.

Roll the labneh into small balls and place in a clean sterilised glass jar.

Cover the labneh with olive oil and seal the lid. Keep refrigerated and the labneh will last for a few weeks.

Serve on a mezze platter or crumble on top of pan-fried mushrooms or a salad.

Sausage rolls

1 lb/500 g beef mince
1 lb/500 g sausage mince
2 cups breadcrumbs
2 carrots, grated
1 zucchini, grated
1 onion, grated
1 tablespoon sage, chopped
1 tablespoon Worcestershire sauce
½ teaspoon Lebanese spice mix (see recipe p. 13 or can be purchased from Middle Eastern grocers)
1 packet of puff pastry (about 5 sheets)
sesame seeds, to garnish

EGG WASH
1 egg
¼ cup milk
salt, to taste

Makes 20

Preheat the oven to 350°F/180°C fan-forced. Line a baking tray with baking paper. Remove the puff pastry from the freezer.

Place all the ingredients, except the puff pastry, sesame seeds and the egg wash, into a bowl and mix well until everything has been combined.

Along the edge of one sheet of puff pastry, place a roll of the sausage filling. Roll the edge of the pastry over the filling and overlap the edge to form a cylinder shape.

Place the long sausage roll onto a chopping board. Cut your sausage rolls to a desired length; I usually make small ones and cut mine about 1 in (½ cm) wide. Place on a lined baking tray.

Whisk all the egg wash ingredients together. Brush the egg wash on top of sausage rolls.

Sprinkle with some sesame seeds. Continue making rolls with the rest of the mixture until all the filling has been used up.

Bake for about 40 minutes or until golden.

You can freeze uncooked sausage rolls on a tray. To reheat, bake them in a moderate oven for 20 minutes or until golden on the outside.

Khiyar bi laban
Cucumber and yoghurt dip

2 cucumbers
1lb/500 g Greek yoghurt
1 small clove garlic, crushed
salt, to taste
small pinch dried mint (dried herbs
   have an intense flavour so be
   careful not to use too much)

Makes 3 small bowls

Grate the cucumber and leave to drain on absorbent paper.

Once the cucumber has drained, mix all the ingredients together in a bowl and taste to adjust the seasoning.

Line a sieve with paper towel and pour the into the sieve.

Place the sieve over a large bowl to drain the yoghurt mixture.

Allow to stand in the fridge overnight.

Once finished, put the dip into a sterilised container. This should last for at least 2 weeks in the fridge.

Carrot dip

1 teaspoon ghee (clarified butter)
2 carrots, peeled and grated
17½ fl oz/500 ml Greek yoghurt
salt, to taste

Makes 3 small bowls

Place a pan on medium heat and melt the ghee. Fry off the carrot until tender (this may only take a few minutes). Remove the pan from the heat and set aside to cool down.

In a bowl, combine the carrot and yoghurt and season with salt to taste.

Place paper towel in a sieve and pour in the yoghurt mixture. Drain the yoghurt over a bowl and leave overnight in the fridge.

The next day, put the carrot dip in a sterilised container. This should last about 2 weeks in the fridge.

My family has had a huge influence on my cooking. My mother's kitchen was out of bounds when I was a child, but once I was older I loved being involved in the chopping, stirring, tasting and creating that went on. My mother would spend the whole day cooking for us. At meal times, my mother would prepare individual meals for me and my two youngest brothers, to keep us happy.

Our Lebanese culture is very generous and hospitable. My parents love having the family over for any occasion and nobody goes away hungry; if you come over for a quick coffee you don't leave until you've had a three-course dinner and dessert. There is always food around to share with people—biscuits, dips, mezze. It doesn't have to be a special occasion to cook for the people you love.

While my mother cooks strictly Lebanese food, I love all Middle Eastern food. Our family is now influenced by more than just Lebanese food. My husband is Egyptian and my brothers, sisters and cousins have married people from Greece, Cyprus and Turkey. As we share the food of our family and our heritage we learn about different cultures. At family gatherings, we share all kinds of Middle Eastern food. That's what I love about Middle Eastern culture—it makes people comfortable and it makes people happy, to share a meal with someone, it brings people together.

Baba ghanouj

Smoky eggplant dip

1 eggplant
1 tablespoon tahini paste
1 clove garlic, crushed
juice of 1 lemon
salt, to taste
good drizzle of olive oil

Serves 2

Char the skin of the eggplant by placing it directly over an open flame on a gas cook top. If you don't have a gas stove, cook the eggplant over a barbecue for 10 minutes, turning over once skin is charred and blistered. Alternatively, you can char the skin off in the oven. Preheat the oven to the hottest setting. Line a baking tray with baking paper. Slice the eggplant in half and place the halves on the baking tray, skin side up. Roast in the oven for about 15 minutes, or until the skin blackens.

Once the skin is blackened, remove from the heat and leave to cool. Once cool enough to handle, peel the eggplant.

Place the eggplant and the remaining ingredients into a blender and combine everything until smooth. Add extra seasoning or lemon juice (1 tablespoon at a time) if you think it needs it.

Mushroom pizza

1 tomato, finely diced

1 green bell pepper/capsicum, finely diced

5 kalamata olives, finely sliced

3 mint leaves, finely shredded

¼ cup mozzarella cheese, grated

¼ cup parmesan cheese, grated

¼ cup feta cheese, grated

2 tablespoons olive oil

5 large mushrooms, stem removed

Makes 5

Preheat the oven to 350°F/180°C fan-forced.

Place the tomato, bell pepper, olives and mint leaves in a bowl and stir to combine.

In a separate bowl, mix together all three cheeses.

Heat the oil in a pan over a medium heat.

Once the oil is hot, place the mushrooms in the pan and fry for 1 minute.

Place the mushrooms on a chopping board with the stem side facing up. Place 1 tablespoon of the tomato mixture into the mushroom cap, then sprinkle with 1 tablespoon of the cheese. Place the mushrooms onto a baking tray lined with baking paper and bake in the oven for 5 minutes until the cheese has melted and is golden.

Smoky eggplant salad

1 eggplant
1 tomato, finely diced
1 bell pepper/capsicum, finely
  diced
1 pomegranate, seeded
2 tablespoons flat-leaf parsley, finely
  chopped
2 tablespoons mint leaves, finely
  chopped
salt, to taste
good drizzle of olive oil
juice of 1 lemon

Serves 4

Char the skin of the eggplant by placing it directly on the gas stovetop over an open flame. If you don't have a gas stove, cook the eggplant over a barbecue for 10 minutes, turning over once skin is charred and blistered. Alternatively, you can char the skin off in the oven. Preheat the oven to the hottest setting. Line a baking tray with baking paper. Slice the eggplant in half and place the halves on the baking tray, skin side up. Roast in the oven for about 15 minutes, or until the skin blackens.

Once the skin is blackened, remove from the heat and leave to cool. Once cool enough to handle, peel the eggplant.

Shred the eggplant with a fork. Place the eggplant and the remaining ingredients into a bowl and stir to combine.

Season to taste, adding more salt or lemon juice as preferred.

Herb crêpes

3 tablespoons mint, finely shredded

3 tablespoons parsley, finely
shredded

3 tablespoons scallions/spring
onion, finely sliced

2 tablespoons parmesan, grated

5 eggs

2 tablespoons milk

5 tablespoons all-purpose/plain flour

salt, to taste

cracked black pepper

drizzle of olive oil, for frying

Makes 6

Mix all the ingredients in a bowl until well combined. If thick, add
1 tablespoon at a time of extra milk to make it into a more runny mixture.

Place a frying pan over a medium heat.

Once the pan is hot, pour 1 ladle of mixture into the pan and swirl the
pan around so the mixture forms a thin even layer.

After 30 seconds, have a sneak peak to see if the bottom of the crêpe is
golden. If so, flip the crêpe over for a further 30 seconds. Once cooked,
set the crêpe aside on a paper towel-lined plate.

Repeat with the remaining ingredients.

Serve these warm with a dollop of yoghurt.

Green olives

This was my great-grandmother's recipe, passed down to my grandma, my mum and now I am passing it on to you.

2 lb 4 oz / 1 kg green olives, smashed with a sterilised stone or in a mortar and pestle
3 lemons
2 whole bird's eye chillies
2 sprigs of thyme
2 lb 4 oz / 1 kg salt
1½ cups olive oil

Makes 1 jar

Give the olives a light smash so they crack open a little. Put the olives in a large sterilised jar and pour in enough water to fill the jar. Add 4 tablespoons of salt and leave for 24 hours. Drain the water, reserving the olives. Rinse and put them back in the same jar with 4 tablespoons salt and enough water to cover them. Leave for another 24 hours. Repeat this salting process two more times.

After the fourth time, drain the eater and place the olives into a separate bowl. Quarter the lemons and put them on top of the olives. Add in the chillies, thyme sprigs and 6 tablespoons of salt. Give everything a good mix. Pour the mixture back into the jar and fill three-quarters of the jar with water then fill the remaining one-quarter of the jar with olive oil. Seal and leave for 2 months before using. This will last up to one year in the jar.

Preserved vegetables

2 tablespoons superfine/caster
  sugar
4 tablespoons salt
1 tablespoon coriander seeds
2 cups white vinegar
½ beetroot
2 turnips, peeled and chopped like
  thick potato chips
2 carrots, sliced 1 in (2 cm) thick
5 long hot green chillies
water

Makes 1 jar

In a bowl, mix together the sugar, salt, coriander seeds and vinegar and stir until the sugar has dissolved.

Pour the pickling liquid into a sterilised jar. Add in the vegetables, then fill the rest with water. Screw on the lid and set aside for at least 2 weeks before using. This will last for up to 4 months.

Mains

باهنا ولاسفا
ياهلزي زيانزي

Crispy fish with parsnip puree and spinach

3 parsnips, diced into ¼ in (1 cm) pieces
10½ fl oz/300 ml thickened cream, plus extra to taste
2 garlic cloves, finely chopped
1 thyme sprig
2½ fl oz/80 ml (¹/3 cup) olive oil
½ onion, finely diced
1 bunch English spinach, washed and roughly chopped
½ lemon, juiced
4 x 6 oz/180 g white-fleshed fish fillets (such as barramundi)
salt and cumin, to taste

Serves 4

Preheat the oven to 350°F/180°C.

To make parsnip puree, place parsnip pieces, cream, half of the garlic, and thyme sprig in a saucepan over medium heat, and bring to the boil. Reduce heat to a simmer, and cook for 15 minutes or until parsnip is tender. Transfer to a blender and process to a puree, adding 1 tablespoon of cream at a time to thin out puree, if necessary. Season with salt and pepper, and set aside.

Heat 2 tablespoons olive oil in a large frying pan over medium heat. Add diced onion and remaining garlic, and cook for 4 minutes or until golden, stirring regularly. Add spinach, reduce the heat and cook until wilted. Stir in lemon juice, salt to taste and set aside.

Heat the remaining 2 tablespoons of oil in an ovenproof frying pan over medium heat. Season the fish with salt and cumin and score the skin twice, place in pan skin-side down, cook for 4 minutes, then transfer to oven to cook for a further 6 minutes or until just cooked through. It is important that you keep it skin side down so you will have crispy skin.

Serve the fish on top of the spinach with parsnip puree on the side.

Barbecue fish with tomato salsa

TOMATO SALSA

3 small vine-ripened tomatoes
2 eschalots, finely chopped
2½ fl oz/75 ml lemon juice
1¾ oz/50 g black olives, pitted,
    quartered
1 teaspoon basil, finely chopped
1 teaspoon cilantro/coriander, finely
    chopped
salt and pepper, to taste

4 fish fillets, pin-boned (snapper or
    another white, lean and flaky fish)
olive oil, for frying plus extra for
    serving

Serves 4

Preheat the oven to 350°F/180°C and line a tray with baking paper.

Bring a saucepan of salted water to the boil over high heat. Make a cross-incision in the base of each tomato. Blanch in boiling water for 20 seconds or until skin is starting to peel at the cross, then plunge into a bowl of iced water to stop the cooking process. Once cool enough to handle, remove skins and seeds, and chop flesh into thin pieces. Set aside.

Heat olive oil in a frying pan over medium heat. Cook eschalots until tender but have not taken on any colour. Remove from heat and stir in lemon juice, tomato, olives, basil and cilantro, and season to taste with salt and pepper. Set aside.

Heat a chargrill pan over high heat or heat up a barbecue. Generously drizzle fish with oil, and season with salt and pepper.

Place the fish in the pan, skin-side down, and cook for 1 minute. Remove from the pan and cook in the oven for 4 mintes.

Alternatively, cook the fish on a barbecue, skin-side down, for about 2 minutes, then carefully turn over and cook for 4 minutes or until just cooked through.

To serve, divide tomato salsa among plates, place fish on top, then spoon over remaining tomato salsa. Drizzle with extra olive oil.

Confit salmon tarator with crispy salmon skin

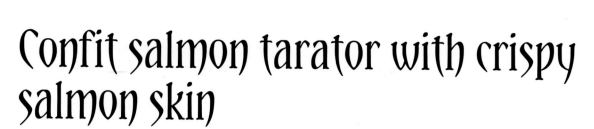

14 fl oz/400 ml olive oil
5 x 4½ oz/130 g salmon fillets
  skin on, pin-boned, at room
  temperature

TARATOR
2½ oz/75 g Greek yoghurt
juice of 1 lemon
2 tablespoons tahini
1 garlic clove, finely chopped
1¾ oz/50 g walnuts, roasted,
  finely chopped
½ bunch cilantro/coriander leaves,
  finely chopped
¼ bunch parsley leaves, finely
  chopped
¼ bunch mint leaves, finely chopped
½ red onion, finely chopped
½ long red chilli, finely chopped
½ teaspoon sumac
drizzle of olive oil
salt, to taste

Serves 5

Preheat the oven to 320°F/160°C and line a tray with baking paper.

Heat oil in a large saucepan to 113°F/45°C (use a thermometer to measure the heat). Heat a large saucepan of water to 113°F/45°C.

Remove the skin from the salmon, then place skin on tray and season well with salt. Cover skin with another piece of baking paper, and place another flat tray on top. Roast in oven for 20 minutes or until skin is very crisp.

Once oil has reached 113°F/45°C, carefully pour 3½ fl oz/100 ml into a double-sealed zip lock or food saver bag, and place one salmon fillet and a generous pinch of salt inside. Seal bag. Repeat process with remaining oil and salmon. Place bags into the water bath for 25 minutes or until the salmon is just cooked through, ensuring the temperature is maintained at 113°F/45°C so you don't overcook the salmon.

For the tarator, combine yoghurt, half the lemon juice, tahini and garlic in a bowl. Season to taste. Combine remaining ingredients in a separate bowl.

To serve, very carefully remove salmon from the bags, and pat dry with paper towel, then place on plates. Smear tarator sauce on top of the salmon fillets. Sprinkle walnut mixture over salmon to coat. Serve with crispy salmon skin.

Note: Tarator is a sauce usually eaten with fish.

Eye fillet with celeriac puree and balsamic jus

2 tablespoons olive oil
4 x 7½ oz/220 g beef eye fillets
freshly ground white pepper, to
    season
salt and pepper, to taste

CELERIAC PUREE
1½ oz/40 g butter
1 small celeriac, peeled and finely
    diced
1 garlic clove, finely chopped
21 fl oz/600 ml thickened cream

BALSAMIC JUS
2 tablespoons olive oil
1 onion, roughly chopped
1 celery stick, roughly chopped
1 carrot, roughly chopped
3½ fl oz/100 ml balsamic vinegar
17½ fl oz/500 ml (2 cups) veal
    stock
1 tablespoon butter, diced

Serves 4

Preheat the oven to 350°F/180°C.

For the celeriac puree, melt butter in a saucepan over medium–low heat. Once foaming, add celeriac and cook for 5 minutes, stirring occasionally. Add garlic and cream and bring to the boil. Reduce heat to a simmer and cook for a further 15 minutes or until celeriac is tender. Drain through a sieve, reserving the cream. Puree celeriac in a blender until smooth, adding 2 tablespoons of the reserved cream. Season to taste with salt and pepper. Transfer to a small saucepan and keep warm. Gently reheat before serving.

For the balsamic jus, heat oil in a saucepan over medium heat. Cook onion, celery and carrot for about 6–8 minutes until caramelised. Add the balsamic vinegar and reduce the liquid by half. Add veal stock and cook for about for 20 minutes or until reduced by half. Strain sauce through a fine sieve into a clean saucepan and place over low heat. Once simmering, whisk in butter, one piece at a time, until combined. Season to taste.

Heat olive oil in a large ovenproof frying pan over high heat. Season steaks with salt and white pepper. Quickly sear steaks until completely caramelised. Place pan into the oven for a further 7 minutes until cooked to medium, or until cooked to your liking. Remove from oven and allow to rest for 5 minutes.

To serve, smear celeriac puree onto plates. Place fillets to the side. Pour jus on top.

Crispy skin duck with pickled baby turnips

1 cup verjus

3 teaspoons superfine/caster sugar

8 baby turnips, washed and halved

17½ fl oz/500 ml beef stock

1 tablespoon olive oil

2 eschalots, finely chopped

1 carrot, chopped

1 clove garlic, chopped

3½ oz/100 g honey

3½ oz/100 g pomegranate
   molasses

1 tablespoon cornflour/cornstarch

salt, to taste

1 cup basmati rice

2 cups water, boiled

4 x 7 oz/200 g duck breasts, skin
   lightly scored

1 teaspoon Lebanese spice mix (see
   recipe p. 13 or can be purchased
   from Middle Eastern grocers)

Serves 4

For the pickled turnips, place verjus and sugar in a small saucepan and bring to the boil over medium heat, stirring to dissolve sugar. Place turnips in a bowl, then pour over the verjus mixture. Set aside for 30 minutes, then drain and set aside.

Meanwhile, bring the stock to the boil in a saucepan over a high heat. Heat oil in a frying pan over medium–high heat. Fry eschalots, carrot and garlic for 3 minutes until golden. Add the honey and pomegranate molasses, and cook for 4 minutes until the mixture has thickened, stirring constantly. Carefully transfer the mixture to the pan with stock, whisking to combine. Bring to the boil and cook for about 20 minutes until reduced by half.

Combine cornflour with 2 teaspoons water in a bowl, then add to the frying pan. Reduce heat to medium heat, stirring until mixture thickens. Strain through a fine sieve, season to taste with salt, set aside and keep warm.

Place one cup of rice in a pot with 2 cups of boiling water. Turn the heat down to a simmer with lid on, salt to taste. Once water is absorbed turn heat off and fluff the rice up and put aside.

Season duck breasts with Lebanese spice mix and salt. Place in a cold frying pan, skin-side down, set over medium–high heat. Cook for 4 minutes until skin is lightly golden and crisp, and the fat has rendered. Carefully drain off excess fat. Turn the breasts over and cook for a further 4 minutes, turning over onto the skin-side for a further 4 minutes until cooked to medium. Set aside and cover, to rest for 10 minutes.

To serve, place steamed rice on plates. Slice duck breasts, place on top of rice, then drizzle with 3 tablespoons of sauce. Scatter with turnip and serve with an arugula and walnut salad (see recipe p. 85).

Dukkah cutlets with eggplant dip and a summer salad

EGGPLANT DIP

1 eggplant
1 tablespoon tahini
½ garlic clove, crushed
½ lemon, juiced
salt, to taste

SUMMER SALAD

1 pomegranate, seeded
2 cucumbers, peeled and slice into
   match sticks
2 tablespoons mint, finely chopped
2 tablespoons cilantro/coriander,
   finely chopped

DUKKAH

1½ tablespoons coriander seeds,
   toasted
1½ tablespoons cumin seeds,
   toasted
6 tablespoons hazelnuts toasted
3 tablespoons pine nuts
1 tablespoon olive oil, plus extra

14 oz/400 g lamb rack, cut into
   double-cutlets
2 tablespoons honey
2 tablespoons pomegranate
   molasses

Serves 3

Preheat the oven to 350°F/180°C.

To make the eggplant dip, char the skin of the eggplant on a gas stove-top. Allow to cool. Alternatively, you can char the skin off in the oven. Preheat the oven to the hottest setting. Line a baking tray with baking paper. Slice the eggplant in half and place the halves on the baking tray, skin side up. Roast in the oven for about 15 minutes, or until the skin blackens. Once cool enough to handle, peel and place the flesh in a blender with tahini, garlic, lemon juice and salt to taste, processing until smooth.

In a dry frying pan, toast the nuts and the spices over a low heat being careful not to burn them. Pound spices in a mortar and pestle until finely ground, then add nuts and coarsely grind.

Heat oil in a frying pan over high heat. Sear lamb for 1–2 minutes until browned. Remove lamb from heat.

Mix honey and pomegranate molasses in a bowl and coat the lamb with the molasses mixture, then roll the lamb in dukkah (reserving 1 tablespoon for garnish). Place lamb in a roasting pan and cook in the oven for 10 minutes until cooked to medium. Set aside to rest.

To make the salad, combine pomegranate seeds (reserving 1 tablespoon for garnish), cucumber, mint and cilantro in a bowl, drizzle with olive oil and toss to combine. Season to taste with salt.

Serve cutlets with dip and salad on the side. Sprinkle with reserved dukkah and pomegranate seeds.

Fatet jaj

Crispy bread chicken with yoghurt and nut topping and pickled carrot and purple cabbage salad

1 tablespoon Lebanese spice mix, plus an extra pinch (see recipe p. 13 or can be purchased from Middle Eastern grocers)

2 tablespoons hot paprika, plus an extra pinch

2 tablespoons salt

6 lb 10 oz/3 kg chicken thighs fillet

2½ oz/80 g ghee

4 lb 6 oz/2 kg Greek yoghurt

1 clove garlic, crushed

flat bread, to serve

3 tablespoons ghee

5 oz/150 g slivered almonds

5 oz/150 g pine nuts

Serves 6

Firstly, combine the spices and salt in a large bowl. Add the chicken and toss to coat. Heat ghee in a large, heavy-based saucepan over medium–high heat. Cook the chicken in batches until golden.

Return all the chicken to pan. Add enough water to just cover the chicken and turn the heat up to a simmer. Season with a pinch of Lebanese spice mix and a good pinch of salt and simmer for 40 minutes or until tender and cooked through. Remove chicken from the liquid and set aside to cool. Increase heat to medium–high and reduce stock by half. Once cool enough to handle, shred the meat and return to stock. Reheat when ready to serve.

In a bowl, combine yoghurt, garlic and salt to taste and refrigerate until needed.

Tear up the flat bread to bite-sized pieces and fry in a pan with 2 tablespoons ghee on medium heat until golden. Place on kitchen paper until needed.

For the nuts, heat the rest of the ghee in a large frying pan over low–medium heat. Cook nuts for about 5 minutes or until toasted. Set aside.

Recipe cont.

SALAD

½ cup (3¾ oz/110 g) superfine/
    caster sugar, plus extra for dressing
2 cups (17½ fl oz/500 ml) white
    vinegar
2 teaspoons salt, plus extra to taste
2 carrots, thinly sliced into
    matchsticks
juice of 2 lemons
½ cup (4 fl oz/125 ml) olive oil
½ red cabbage, shredded
1 bunch mint, leaves picked
1 bunch cilantro/coriander, leaves
    picked

Serves 6

To make the salad, whisk sugar, vinegar and 2 teaspoons salt in a bowl until sugar has dissolved. Add carrots and refrigerate for at least 30 minutes to pickle.

For the dressing, whisk lemon juice, olive oil, salt to taste in a large bowl until salt has dissolved.

When ready to serve, rinse and drain carrots, pat dry with paper towel. Add carrot, cabbage and herbs to a bowl with dressing and toss to combine. Set aside until needed.

To serve, layer fried flatbread in a large shallow serving plate, top with a ladle of chicken and drizzle with 4 tablespoons of the reduced stock. Serve the yoghurt and nuts in separate bowls alongside. Once you've dished up everyone's serving, pour the yoghurt over the chicken and sprinkle with some nuts.

Makloubeh

Upside down rice

2 lb 4 oz/1 kg shoulder of lamb
Lebanese spice mix (see recipe
   p. 13 or can be purchased from
   Middle Easter grocers)
salt
4 eggplants, peeled and cut into
   1 cm round slices
canola oil, for roasting
2 lb 4 oz/1 kg white medium grain
   rice
1½ oz/40 g ghee (clarified butter)
1 cup slivered almonds
1 cup pine nuts
36 fl oz/1 litre Greek yoghurt

Serves 7

Preheat the oven to 350°F/180°C.

Put lamb in a pot filled with water over a medium-high heat. Bring to a boil and scoop the scum off the top as it comes to the top. Boil for 10 minutes before removing from the heat. Rinse the lamb and put it back into a clean pot with enough water to cover the lamb and season with salt and 2 teaspoons of Lebanese spice mix and a pinch of black pepper. Bring to a boil then reduce the heat and simmer, uncovered, for 2 hours or until the meat is very tender and falling apart. Top up with water if needed. Remove from the heat and leave in the stock.

Peel and slice the eggplant to 1 cm thickness. Season with salt and put aside for 10 minutes to sweat it out. Place the eggplant on an oven tray with a good drizzle of canola oil and roast in the oven until golden. Turn over after 15 minutes and cook until both sides are golden. You can fry the eggplant in butter or oil, if you prefer.

Once the lamb is tender, taste the liquid and make sure the seasoning is right. This will be the stock you cook your rice in.

Layer the lamb in the bottom of an ovenproof casserole dish then layer over the eggplant and then scatter with rice. Pour the hot stock (the liquid the lamb was cooking in) over the entire dish. You need enough liquid to just cover the rice.

Recipe cont.

Bring to a boil then turn down the heat, cover and leave to simmer for 30 minutes until the rice is tender and all the liquid has been absorbed.

Once all the liquid has been absorbed, put a tray or a large chopping board on top of the pot. Make sure the tray is larger then the pot. Flip the pot over into the tray and give it a tap, lift the pot off and you should have a layer of meat then eggplant then rice.

Place a large saucepan on medium heat. Add the ghee and, once melted, add the nuts and constantly stir until golden. Then pour the nuts and some of the ghee over the makloubeh.

Note: I love eating this dish with yoghurt.

Pickled beetroot, avocado and arugula with poached egg

17½ fl oz/500 ml white vinegar
    plus extra ¼ cup vinegar
4 tablespoons superfine/caster
    sugar
1 teaspoon coriander seeds
1 cup water
1 bunch baby beetroot, washed and
    stems removed
1 avocado, skin and stone removed
½ lemon juice
salt
1 tomato, diced
handful of arugula/rocket
2 eggs, poached
pinch of Dukkah (see recipe p. 32)

Serves 2

Put the vinegar, sugar, coriander seeds, water and beetroots in a pot over a medium heat and bring to a boil. Lower the heat and simmer for 20 minutes until tender.

Place the avocado flesh, lemon juice and pinch of salt into a blender and blend until smooth.

Transfer the avocado to a bowl and fold the diced tomato through.

Bring a pot of water to the boil and add in ¼ cup of vinegar. While the water is boiling, crack the eggs into the water and allow to simmer for 1½ minutes. Remove the eggs with a slotted spoon. If you like your eggs hard-boiled, leave in for a few minutes.

To serve, arrange some avocado puree, beetroots and some rocket on a plate and place the poached egg on top. Sprinkle with the dukkah.

Spatchcock stuffed with moghrabiya date and carrot puree

1 tablespoon baharat spice mix (see recipe p. 20 or can be purchased from Middle Eastern grocers)

7 oz/200 g (1 cup) moghrabieh (large couscous)

8 pitted dates, finely chopped

3½ oz/100 g pistachios

4 tablespoons cilantro/coriander, finely chopped

3½ oz/100 g ghee (clarified butter)

1 duck breast, skin removed, finely diced

¼ teaspoon salt

4 x 1 lb/500 g spatchcocks

½ teaspoon cayenne pepper

1½ oz/40 g butter

2 carrots, peeled, roughly chopped

5½ fl oz/160 ml beef stock

pinch saffron

salt, to taste

cilantro/coriander leaves, to garnish

Serves 4

Combine cumin, allspice, black pepper, cloves and nutmeg in a bowl.

Bring a saucepan of water to the boil. Add moghrabieh and cook for 15 minutes or until tender. Put through a sieve and rinse under running water, then transfer to a bowl. Add 1 teaspoon of the spice mixture, dates, pistachios, cilantro, 1½ oz/40 g ghee, duck and ¼ teaspoon salt to the couscous and stir well to combine.

Stuff spatchcocks with the couscous stuffing and close with a toothpick. Place spatchcocks in a large roasting pan. Add cayenne pepper and 1½ oz/40 g ghee to remaining spice mixture, and stir well to combine. Rub ghee mixture over spatchcocks to coat. Place in oven for 40 minutes or until spatchcocks are golden and juices run clear when a skewer is inserted in between the leg and the thigh.

Meanwhile, melt the butter in a saucepan over medium heat. Add carrots and cook for 1–2 minutes until carrot is coated but do not brown. Add 10½ fl oz/300 ml beef stock and saffron and bring to the boil. Reduce heat to a simmer and cook for 15 minutes or until carrot is tender. Strain the carrot, reserving the stock. Transfer the carrot to a blender and add 2 tablespoons at a time of stock to make a thick puree. Process until smooth. Season with salt to taste, set aside and keep warm.

To serve, smear carrot puree on to the plate and top with a spoonful of stuffing, scooped from the spatchcock. Carve the spitchcock and place on top of the stuffing. Garnish with crispy duck skin and some cilantro leaves.

Turkish lentil soup

3 tablespoons olive oil
2 onions, diced
2 carrots, peeled and diced
2 potatoes, peeled and diced
2½ cups red lentils, rinsed
36 fl oz/1 litre beef stock
17½ fl oz/500 ml boiled water
salt and pepper, to taste

Serves 4

Place a 4 litre pot on medium heat and add the oil.

When the pot is warm, add the onion and stir until it becomes translucent.

Then add your carrots and potato and stir for 30 seconds. Add the lentils and give it a stir.

Add the beef stock and water and bring to the boil. Lower the heat and simmer, stirring every 10 minutes until the lentils and vegetables are very tender and soft. Strain the soup, reserving the liquid.

Put all the solids from the sieve into the blender and blend for 1 minute until it turns all the vegetables into a puree.

Transfer the puree back into the pot, season with salt and pepper. You can adjust the thickness of the soup with the leftover stock. Add half a cup at a time to the desired thickness. I usually like to add about 1 cup of stock to mine. Give it a quick boil and season with salt and cracked pepper to taste.

Corn and zucchini fritters with goat's cheese

1 large green zucchini, grated
1 corn cob, boiled for ten minutes
    (or 3½ oz/100 g frozen or
    canned corn)
½ cup milk
½ cup self-rising/self-raising flour
1 egg
¼ cup goat's feta, crumbled into
    chunks
pinch of salt
canola oil spray

Serves 4

Remove the corn kernels from the cob and place all of the ingredients, except the oil spray, in a large bowl and give it a good mix.

Place a saucepan on a medium heat. Spray with canola oil. Once the pan is hot, pour a ladleful of the mixture into the pan and spread out into a thin even layer. Leave for 50 seconds or until the bottom of the fritter is golden. If your heat is too high and it is too dark, lower the heat.

Carefully turn the fritter over and give it a gentle press. Leave it for a further 50 seconds or until golden.

Set fritter aside on paper towel and repeat process with the rest of the fritter mixture.

Serve these with Khiyar bi laban (see recipe) and a salad.

Shish barak

Middle Eastern dumplings with yoghurt and cilantro soup

DUMPLINGS

1 cup all-purpose/plain flour plus
   extra for dusting
pinch salt
5 tablespoons ghee
3 onions, finely diced
½ kg lamb mince
salt and pepper, to taste
2 cups warm water

YOGHURT SOUP

17½ fl oz/1 litre Greek yoghurt
1 tablespoon cornflour/corn starch
3.6 pints/1.7 litres boiling water
1 egg

1 bunch of cilantro/coriander, finely
   shredded
3 cloves garlic, crushed
salt, to taste

Serves 4

For the dumplings, combine the flour, salt and water in a bowl and mix well to combine. Turn the dough out onto a floured bench and knead for 10 minutes, adding more flour if the dough is too wet. Allow to rest for 15 minutes.

Heat 1 tablespoon of ghee in a medium-sized pan on a high heat. Once melted, add the onion, lamb and seasoning and cook for 10 minutes or until all the liquid has disappeared.

Roll out the dough 3 mm thin. Use a small pastry cutter and cut circles into the dough.

Strain the lamb mixture so no liquid is left and place a teaspoon of mixture onto a pastry circle. Fold the pastry in half, into a moon shape, and pinch the edges together. Repeat with the remaining lamb mince and dough.

Place the yoghurt in a large saucepan and create a well in the centre.

Mix the cornflour with ½ cup of cold water until it is completely mixed together, with no lumps. Add that to the yoghurt.

With a whisk, mix the cornflour and yoghurt together until all combined. Place the pan on the stovetop over a high heat and keep stirring, anti-clockwise. It is VERY important that you do only stir in the same direction. If you don't, you will split the yoghurt and it will look and taste awful. Keep stirring and pour the boiling water into the pot, still stirring in the one direction, without stopping. Once the yoghurt comes to a rapid boil, lower the heat to allow the yoghurt to simmer while still stirring. Put 20 dumplings in the pot and turn the heat back up to high. Once it comes to a boil again you can stop stirring and place on a simmer.

Add 4 tablespoons to a frying pan over medium heat. Once it melts add the garlic and cilantro and fry it off for 1 minute until it becomes very fragrant. Pour this mixture on top of your yoghurt soup. Allow to simmer for 10 minutes, then taste and adjust salt if necessary. Turn off the heat.

To serve, place 6 dumplings or as many as you like in a bowl and pour over the yoghurt soup.

Spicy chicken with an arugula and walnut salad

5 bird's eye chillies

1 red bell pepper/capsicum, roasted, skin removed

2 teaspoons ground cumin

1 teaspoon cinnamon

1 teaspoon salt

juice of 1 lemon

¼ cup olive oil

2 whole chickens, cut into 6 pieces (ask your butcher to do this)

5 oz/150 g ghee

SALAD

3 large handfuls arugula/rocket

1 cup roasted walnuts, roughly chopped

½ cup feta

good drizzle of balsamic vinegar

good drizzle of olive oil

Serves 6–8

Preheat the oven to 350°F/180°C.

Place the chillies, bell pepper, cumin, cinnamon, salt, lemon juice in a blender and process until smooth. While blender is on, pour in the olive oil in a very slow stream. In a large bowl, pour the chilli mixture on top of the chicken, making sure it is all coated, and allow to marinate for at least 30 minutes.

Place a large frying pan on a high heat with half of the ghee and pan-fry the chicken in batches until it is golden in colour. Once pan-fried, transfer the chicken to an oven tray. Melt the rest of the ghee and pour it over the chicken. Roast in the oven for 30 minutes or until the chicken is cooked through.

To make the salad, combine the arugula, walnuts and feta in a bowl and drizzle with balsamic and olive oil. Toss to combine.

To serve, arrange the salad on a serving platter and place the chicken on top.

Kibbeh nahyeh

Middle Eastern tartare

1 lamb back strap, finely chopped
¼ cup fine bulgur
salt, to taste
pepper, to taste
¼ cup olive oil

TOPPING
1 bell pepper/capsicum, roughly
   chopped
½ onion, roughly chopped
1 cup basil leaves
½ cup walnuts
1 bird's eye chilli
salt, to taste

Serves 2

Place the lamb in a blender and blend for 40 seconds until minced. Place in a bowl until needed.

In a separate bowl, add the bulgur and soak in enough water to cover it for 2 minutes. Strain off the water and set aside until needed.

In a clean blender, place all of the topping ingredients and blend until combined into a paste. It's fine if the nuts still have texture.

Put the lamb in a bowl and scatter the bulgur on top. Sprinkle with salt and pepper and 1 tablespoon of the bell pepper puree. Drizzle with the olive oil and mix well. Keep adding oil until the mixture becomes wet.

To serve, spread the kibbeh mixture onto a platter and smear the capsicum paste on top to cover the meat. Enjoy with some flatbread.

Watermelon and feta salad

½ watermelon, chopped into
   triangles
1 cup feta
½ cup mint leaves, finely shredded

Serves 4

Place watermelon onto a platter.
   Crumble the feta cheese on top and garnish with the mint leaves.

Watermelon and halva salad

½ watermelon, roughly chopped
2 tablespoons orange blossom water
½ cup halva with pistachio
½ cup mint leaves

Serves 4

Place the watermelon onto a platter. Sprinkle the orange blossom water on top of the watermelon.
   Crumble the halva over the watermelon and garnish with mint leaves.

Turkish kofta with potato in a spicy tomato sauce

2 lb 4 oz/1 kg lamb mince (the
mince has to be fatty)

2 tablespoons red pepper/capsicum
paste (purchased from Middle
Eastern grocers)

4 tablespoons parsley, finely
shredded

salt, to taste

1 teaspoon fine chilli powder

7 fresh tomatoes

6 baby chat potatoes, peeled and
thickly sliced

2 tablespoons ghee

pinch of Lebanese Spice mix (see
recipe p.13)

cumin, to taste

salt, to taste

Serves 4

Preheat the oven to 350°F/180°C. Line a tray with baking paper.

Combine the lamb, red pepper paste, parsley, salt and chilli in a bowl
and mix well. Once mixed, take 1 tablespoon amount and roll it out
into an oval shape and place on a lined tray. Repeat with the rest of the
mixture then place the tray of kofta in the fridge until needed.

In a blender, blend the tomatoes and then strain through a sieve,
discarding the solids.

Place a large pan on a high heat. Once the pan is hot, heat
1 tablespoon of ghee and fry off the kofta in batches. Once all the kofta
have been fried, place in a deep ovenproof baking dish.

Fry off the potato with 1 tablespoon of ghee and place on top of the
kofta in the ovenproof baking dish.

Pour the tomato puree over the top. Add a pinch of Lebanese spice mix,
pinch of cumin and season with salt. Bake in the oven for 30 minutes until
the potato is tender and the kofta is cooked through.

Serve this straight from the baking dish with bread or rice.

Stuffed zucchini in a tomato sauce

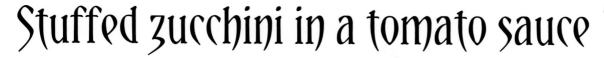

You will need a zucchini or apple corer for this recipe, which you can purchase from a Middle Eastern grocer.

10 Lebanese zucchini (marrows)

STUFFING
7 oz/200 g lamb mince
1 cup medium grain uncooked rice
1 teaspoon salt
½ teaspoon Lebanese Spice mix
   (see recipe p. 13)
¼ cup pine nuts
2 tablespoons ghee

SAUCE
2 tablespoons tomato paste
1 teaspoon Lebanese spice mix (see
   recipe p. 13)
2 teaspoons salt

Serves 2

Cut the tops off the zucchini and core all of them without breaking or putting a hole through the other side.

Mix the lamb, rice, salt and Lebanese spice mix together in a bowl.

Heat a saucepan over a medium heat and melt the ghee. Fry the pine nuts until golden then pour the pine nuts and ghee on top of the lamb mixture. Mix everything together.

Loosely stuff the zucchini with the rice mixture, so that the zucchini are three-quarters full.

To make the sauce, cook the tomato paste in a large saucepan on a high heat for 30 seconds. Fill up with 67½ fl oz/2 litres of water. Once it comes to the boil, add the zucchini, the Lebanese spice mix and the salt. Bring to a boil then turn the heat down and simmer for 45 minutes. Taste the stock and adjust the seasoning if necessary.

Remove the zucchini from the sauce and serve on a plate with a drizzle of the tomato sauce over the top.

If you aren't going to be eating this straight away, store the zucchini and sauce separately. If you are reheating it, put the zucchini back in the tomato sauce and boil for 10 minutes before serving

Fried kibbeh

2 lb 4 oz/1 kg fine bulgur

2 bunch basil leaves

2 red bell peppers/capsicums, roughly chopped

2 onions, roughly chopped

1 hot red chilli, roughly chopped

2 lb 4 oz/1 kg kibbeh lamb mince (or 2 lb 4 oz/1 kg lamb back straps blended for 1 minute into a fine mince)

1 tablespoon salt, or to taste

2 teaspoons Lebanese Spice mix (see recipe p. 13)

FILLING

2 tablespoons ghee

2 lb 4 oz/1 kg lamb mince

4 large onions, finely diced

1 cup pine nuts

3 tablespoons pomegranate molasses (optional)

Makes 60

Soak the bulgur in water for 5 minutes. Strain through a sieve.

In a blender, add the basil leaves, bell peppers, onion and chilli and blend to a fine puree.

In a large bowl, add the kibbeh meat and red bell pepper puree. Mix together, then add the bulgur, salt and spice mix. Mix well with your hands. Add ¼ cup of water at a time and keep mixing well until soft—not stiff or runny. I usually add 1½ cups water, but this will depend on the type of bulgur you've used.

To make the filling, place a frying pan on a medium heat and melt 2 tablespoons of ghee, then add the minced meat and onion. Season with salt and cook for 10 minutes until cooked through and there is no liquid left.

In a separate frying pan, toast the pine nuts then scatter over the lamb and onion mixture. Add the pomegranate molasses now, if using. Give the mixture a stir and leave to cool.

Put a bowl of water beside you to wet your hands as you roll the kibbeh mixture. Roll out golf ball sized balls of the mixture and place them onto a lined tray—this should make around 30 kibbeh balls.

Hold the ball in your left hand and place your right index finger in the ball then rotate to hollow the ball out without going right through. Fill with the mince mixture and seal the top of the kibbeh. Once you've stuffed the kibbeh, the balls can be frozen and used at a later date without defrosting.

Heat some oil in a large, deep saucepan and deep-fry until golden on the outside, about 5 minutes. Remove the cooked balls with a slotted spoon and set aside on a plate covered with paper towel to drain.

Serve on a platter with plain yoghurt for dipping.

Delaa wa rez

Chicken lemon soup with vermicelli rice

2 tablespoons ghee
2 lb 4 oz/1 kg Maryland chicken
    fillets (whole leg with thigh and
    drumstick)
1 teaspoon Lebanese Spice mix (see
    recipe p. 13)
1 teaspoon hot paprika
juice of 7 lemons
2 teaspoons salt

RICE
3 tablespoons ghee
1 cup vermicelli, broken
2 cups medium grain rice
2 teaspoons salt
4 cups boiling water

Serves 4

Cut the chicken in quarters then place the chicken pieces, Lebanese spice mix and hot paprika in a bowl and mix well

Melt the ghee in a large pot over a high heat. Fry off the chicken in batches, until golden. Once all of the chicken has been browned, return it all to the pot and fill with water until the chicken is covered by 1 in (2 cm) of water.

Bring the water to a boil then add the lemon juice and salt. Reduce the heat and simmer for 40 minutes, until the chicken is falling off the bone. Check the seasoning is right. Set aside until the rice is cooked.

To make the rice, place a 101 fl oz/3 litre pot on high heat. Melt the ghee and add the vermicelli. Constantly stir until golden. Add the rice and salt and stir to coat all the rice with the ghee. Add the water and bring to a boil then cover and lower the heat to a simmer for 20 minutes, or until all the liquid has been absorbed.

Allow to stand for 10 minutes before serving. Do not stir during the absorbtion process and resting time.

The traditional way to serve this is to place 2 ladlefuls of rice into a bowl and in a separate bowl place the chicken and soup. I personally prefer my rice, chicken and soup directly on top of each other in the same bowl. This soup tastes lemony but delicious.

Samkeh hara with sayadiyah

Tangy chilli snapper with a nutty rice

36 fl oz/1 litre canola oil, for frying
2 x 1 lb/500 g whole snapper,
  cleaned and scaled
2 teaspoons salt
2 bunches cilantro/coriander, finely
  shredded
1 cup walnuts, roughly chopped
4 cloves garlic, crushed
2 tablespoons dried chilli flakes
juice of 6 lemons

RICE
1 large onion, finely diced
¼ cup pine nuts
1 cup medium grain rice
2 teaspoons salt

Serves 4

Heat the oil to 375°F/190°C.

Score the snapper three times on an angle. Season fish with salt on the outside and the inside.

Deep-fry for 5 minutes until just cooked through. Place on some paper towel to drain excess oil. Reserve the oil in the pan to cook the rice with later.

For the filling, in a bowl, mix together the cilantro, walnuts, garlic and chilli. Rub this mixture into the fish and stuff the inside with it. Set aside until needed.

To prepare the rice, heat 1 cup of the reserved oil over a high heat, add the onion and cook until it is dark brown. Add 2 cups of water, bring to a boil and boil for ten minutes. Strain, reserving the liquid and discarding the onion. Keep the liquid to cook the rice.

In a 67 fl oz/2-litre pot, toast the pine nuts on a medium heat until golden. Add the rice and salt then add the onion liquid and bring to a boil. Turn down the heat, cover and simmer until all the liquid has been absorbed and the rice is cooked through. Take the rice off the heat and leave for
10 minutes, covered, but do not stir.

Place the snapper and lemon juice in a baking dish and bring to a boil on low–medium heat for 2 minutes to warm through.

Stir the onions through the rice. On a platter, spread out the rice, place the snapper on top and enjoy.

Lamb tagine

1 bunch cilantro/coriander, stalks and leaves roughly chopped
3 cloves garlic, chopped
1 in/2 cm knob ginger, peeled and chopped
1 bird's eye chilli,
1 large onion, roughly chopped
2 tablespoons ghee (clarified butter)
2 lb 4 oz/1 kg shoulder of lamb, diced into small pieces
1 eggplant, diced into large pieces
1 zucchini, diced into large pieces
1 tomato, roughly diced
1 cup pitted dates
¼ cup raisins
1 teaspoon ras el hanout spice mix (see recipe p. 21 or can be purchased at Middle Eastern grocers)
2 teaspoons salt, to taste
17 fl oz/500 ml beef stock
½ bunch cilantro/coriander, finely shredded, to serve

COUSCOUS
2 cups couscous
2 cups chicken stock
1 teaspoon salt
¼ cup toasted pistachio

Serves 4

Place cilantro, garlic, ginger, chilli and onion in a blender and blend for 40 seconds.

Heat the ghee in a 4-litre pot over a high heat. Season lamb with salt and fry in batches until it is sealed all over. Remove from pan and leave to rest.

In the same pot, place the cilantro mix from the blender and cook for 2 minutes on medium heat until fragrant. Add the lamb and toss to combine.

Add the eggplant, zucchini, tomato, dates and raisins and cook for 3 minutes, stirring to combine.

Add the ras el hanout and salt, give the ingredients a toss then pour in the beef stock. Bring to a boil then lower the heat to a simmer. Simmer, covered, for 2 hours to slow cook, stirring regularly, until the meat is very tender and falls apart when you touch it. If you find the liquid has dried out during the cooking process, add ½ cup of water at a time so the mixture does not burn.

About 10 minutes before the tagine is ready, place the couscous into a large heat-proof bowl. Bring the chicken stock to a boil then pour on top of the couscous, add 1 teaspoon salt, give the couscous a stir, cover with a lid and leave for 15 minutes until all the liquid has been absorbed. Fluff the couscous with a fork, add the toasted pistachio and toss everything together.

To assemble, pour the couscous onto a large platter and serve the lamb tagine on top. Garnish with cilantro just before serving.

Koshari

7 fresh large ripe tomatoes

2 tablespoons ghee

¼ cup vermicelli

1 cup long-grain rice

salt, to taste

½ cup pasta (any type as long as it's
  small)

5 large brown onions, finely diced

2 cups canola oil

2 cloves garlic, peeled, cut in half

¼ cup dried brown lentils

1 x 14 oz/400 g can chickpeas/
  garbanzo beans, drained

chilli sauce (optional)

½ lemon, cut in half, to serve

Serves 4

Put the tomatoes in a blender and blend until pureed. Push the puree through a sieve and reserve the liquid. Set aside.

Melt the ghee in a large saucepan over a high heat. Add the vermicelli and fry until golden. Do not stop stirring or it will burn. Add the rice, a pinch of salt and 2 cups boiling water. Stir everything and reduce the heat to a simmer. Cover with a lid and cook until the rice is tender and all the liquid has been absorbed and the rice is fragrant and tender, about 20 minutes. Remove from the heat and set aside until needed.

In a separate saucepan, bring 2 cups of water to a boil, add the pasta and a pinch of salt and cook until tender. Strain and rinse the pasta. Set aside.

Heat the canola oil in a pan over a high heat. Once hot, fry off the onion until medium brown then carefully strain the onion through a sieve, saving the oil. Drain the onion on a paper towel and leave to dry out. This will be your crispy onion. Using the same pan, bring the tomato liquid and garlic to a boil and boil for 10 minutes or the sauce has thickened a little. Season with salt then take off the heat.

In a very large bowl, add the rice, ¼ cup of the reserved oil, crispy onion, the pasta, lentils and chickpeas. Toss with clean hands until combined.

Put 2 ladlefuls of the mixture in each bowl to serve. Sprinkle with the crispy onion, drizzle with the tomato sauce, sprinkle some chilli sauce on top and squeeze a wedge of lemon over the rice.

Desserts

باطهنا ولا السفا
أنتا حاجك لحاجو لح

Modern baklava

Shortcrust pastry
1½ cups (9 oz/250 g) all-purpose/
  plain flour
4 oz/125 g butter, chilled and
  chopped
⅓ cup confectioner's/icing sugar
1 egg yolk
1 tablespoon milk

SALTED CARAMEL
1 cup dark brown sugar
4 oz/125 g salted butter, diced
4 oz/125 g condensed milk (about
  ½ x 9 oz/250 g can)
1 teaspoon salt, to taste

MOHALABIYA (eggless set custard)
17½ fl oz/500 ml milk
17½ fl oz/500 ml cream
2 tablespoons cornflour/cornstarch
3 tablespoons superfine/caster
  sugar
1 teaspoon orange blossom water
2 cups cashews, dry roasted

Makes 2 large tarts or 8 4 in/8 cm
tarts

To make the pastry, combine flour, butter and sugar in a food processor. Process until the mixture resembles fine breadcrumbs. Add yolk and milk. Process until dough just comes together.

Turn pastry onto a lightly floured surface. Knead until just smooth. Shape into a disc. Wrap in cling film and rest in the refrigerator for 30 minutes.
  Preheat the oven to 350°F/180°C.
  Line a large pastry case with baking paper.
  Place pastry between two baking paper sheets and roll out with a rolling pin to ½ cm thickness. Place into the pastry case, pressing around the edges and then prick the base with a fork a few times. Place the baking paper on top, fill with weights or uncooked rice. Blind bake for 10 minutes. Remove the weights and paper then bake for a further 5 to 10 minutes or until pastry is golden. Allow to cool.

Place a saucepan onto a high heat and add the sugar and 2 tablespoons of water. Once melted and just before it hits burning point, add the butter and condensed milk to the pan, stirring until everything is combined. Add the salt and taste. Be careful as it is very hot. If you cannot taste the salt, sprinkle a little more in.

Place 2 ladlefuls of the salted caramel in the bottom of the cooled tart base. Place in refrigerator to cool.

Place a saucepan over a high heat. Add the milk, cream, cornflour, sugar and orange blossom water and whisk until it comes to a boil and thickens. Pour a layer of mohalabiya onto the cooled caramel in the tart case until it is about 1 cm thick. Sprinkle the cashews on top until the whole layer is covered with the roasted cashews, then drizzle some more salted caramel on top. Place in the fridge for 2 hours before serving to set the mohalabiya.

Spiced sticky date pudding with butterscotch sauce

2½ cups dates, pitted and chopped

2 teaspoons baking soda/
  bicarbonate of soda

21 fl oz/600 ml boiling water

4 oz/125 g unsalted butter,
  softened

1 cup brown sugar

4 eggs

3 cups self-raising flour

1 teaspoon cinnamon

BUTTERSCOTCH SAUCE

10½ fl oz/300 ml full cream

4 oz/125 g unsalted butter

1 cup dark brown sugar

Makes 15

Preheat the oven to 320°F/160°C. Spray two 12-hole muffin tins with oil.

Place the dates, baking soda and the boiling water into a bowl. Stir and cover with cling film then set aside for later.

Place butter and the brown sugar in a bowl. Beat with an electric mixer for about 30 seconds or until combined and fluffy.

Beat in the eggs, one at a time. Keeping the mixer on a medium speed, beat for an extra 1 minute, until everything is smooth and combined.

Sift in the flour and the cinnamon and fold into the mixture, turning the mixer to a low speed. It may look dry but keep beating until the mixture resembles a dough.

Pour the date mixture directly on top of the dough and beat together for about 3 minutes on a medium–high speed.

Fill the muffin tray with the mixture, to three-quarters full. Bake in the oven for 15–20 minutes until golden on top.

Meanwhile, place a saucepan over a high heat and combine all three butterscotch sauce ingredients. Bring to the boil, stirring occasionally. Once boiling, reduce heat and simmer for 5 minutes on low until it thickens. Set aside.

Once the puddings are cooked, remove from the oven and prick a hole in the middle with a skewer. Spoon 1 tablespoon of syrup on top of the pudding and allow to rest for 10 minutes so the cake absorbs the syrup, before serving.

To serve, place the pudding on a plate, pour 2 tablespoons of the butterscotch sauce on top and enjoy with a scoop of vanilla ice cream.

Katayef

Cheese-filled pancakes with a sugar syrup

These are traditionally filled with nabulsi cheese, a white brine cheese, which goes stretchy when heated. A mixture of ricotta and mozzarella has been subsituted here. The mozzarella needs to be soaked for a day before using to remove the salt brine.

3½ cups all-purpose/plain flour
2 tablespoons superfine/caster sugar
1 teaspoon baking powder
pinch of salt
4 cups milk
3 cups grated sweet cheese
ghee or oil, for frying
finely ground pistachio, for garnish

SUGAR SYRUP
1 tablespoon rose water
1 tablespoon orange blossom water
juice of ½ lemon
14 oz/400 g sugar
3 tablespoons water
7 oz/200 g ghee, for frying

Makes 15

In a large bowl, mix together the flour, sugar, baking powder and salt then whisk in the milk to make a runny pancake batter. Sieve the mixture to make sure there are no lumps.

Rest for 2 hours with a tea towel over the bowl.

Place all the sugar syrup ingredients in a saucepan and bring to a boil over a high heat until everything has dissolved and thickened.

Melt a small amount of ghee or oil in a heavy-based pan over a medium heat. Once pan is hot, pour in a ladleful of batter. Once the top of the pancake is bubbling on top, take it out and throw it away—the first 2 you make will not work! They are just testers to make sure the pan is hot enough. If the batter is too thick, add more milk and give it a good mix.

Cook the rest of the batter in the same way. When the pancakes start to bubble on one side—you don't flip these pancakes—and are golden underneath remove from the pan and set them out separately on top of a kitchen towel to cool.

Fill your pancakes with the cheese. Fold in half and pinch the edge together with your fingers to seal.

Place a wide pan on a high heat. Melt 3 tablespoons of ghee in the pan and fry the pancakes for a minute on each side.

Drizzle each hot katayef with sugar syrup.

To serve, place the katayef on a serving plate and sprinkle with the ground pistachio. Serve warm.

Mohalabiya
Eggless set custard

17½ fl oz/500 ml milk
17½ fl oz/500 ml cream
1¾ oz/50 g cornstarch/cornflour
3 tablespoons sugar

SUGAR SYRUP
3½ oz/130 g superfine/caster
  sugar
1 tablespoons orange blossom water
juice of ½ lemon
3 tablespoons water

TOPPING
2 tablespoons dry roasted
  pistachios, unsalted
2 tablespoons shredded coconut
2 tablespoons sultanas

Makes 15

In a saucepan, over a high heat, whisk the milk, cream, cornflour and sugar until it thickens. Pour the mixture through a sieve, to make sure there are no lumps.

Pour the mixture into single cups or shallow plates and place in the refrigerator to set overnight.

To make the sugar syrup, bring the sugar, orange blossom water, lemon juice and water to boil and boil for 7 minutes. Once it has thickened, drizzle 1 tablespoon on top of each mohalabiya. Decorate with the pistachios, coconut and sultanas before serving.

Ghraybeh

Shortbread filled with date and pistachio

9 oz/250 g ghee (cold)
1 cup confectioner's/icing sugar
½ teaspoon baking powder
2 cups all-purpose/plain flour

DATE MIX
7 dates, pitted and chopped
1 cup water
1 tablespoon rose water
1 cup unsalted, roasted pistachios,
  roughly chopped
1 tablespoon superfine/caster sugar
1 tablespoon orange blossom water

Makes 15

Place the ghee in a cake mixer on medium speed and beat until light and fluffy. Slowly add the confectioner's sugar, one spoon at a time. Add the baking powder then slowly add the flour until it forms a dough. Turn the dough out onto a lightly floured bench and pull it together without over working the shortbread dough.

Place the dates and water in a saucepan over a high heat and bring to a boil for 10 minutes. Pour the softened dates and liquid into a blender, add the rosewater and blend to form a puree. Strain the mixture, making sure there are no lumps, then place the smooth date puree in the fridge to cool.

Place the pistachios in a bowl, sprinkle with the sugar and orange blossom water and stir to combine.

Preheat the oven to 400°F/200°C fan-forced. Line a large baking tray with baking paper.

Get 1 tablespoon of the shortbread mix and form it into the shape of a ball. Make an indent using your index finger in the centre of the ball. Fill this with 1 teaspoon of the dates and 1 teaspoon of the pistachio mixture. Close the hole, covering the filling and place onto the baking tray. Make sure you leave 1 in/3 cm gaps between them on the tray. Bake in the oven for 10–15 minutes until they are lightly golden. Take the biscuits out of the oven and allow to rest until cooled.

Awamat

Lebanese doughnuts

2 cups self-raising flour, sifted
1 teaspoon dried yeast
2 tablespoons superfine/caster
   sugar
2 cups warm water
pinch of salt
1 litre corn oil, for frying

SUGAR SYRUP
1 tablespoon rose water
1 tablespoon orange blossom water
juice of ½ lemon
1 lb/500 g superfine/caster sugar
3 tablespoons water

Makes 30

Place the flour, yeast and sugar in a bowl and mix well.

Add in the warm water, whisking well to combine. Pour the mixture through a sieve to make sure there are no lumps (it should be a pancake consistency).

Cover the bowl with cling film. Place a few kitchen towels over it or, even better a blanket, and keep in a warm place for 2 hours.

In the meantime, place all sugar syrup ingredients into a saucepan and bring to a boil and boil for a few minutes until the syrup has thickened and all sugar has dissolved. Take off the heat and set aside.

After 2 hours, heat the oil in a large saucepan over a high heat and place one tablespoon of the doughnut mixture a few at a time into the oil. They will quickly rise to the surface and once golden all over, remove and place directly into the sugar syrup for a few minutes to soak in the syrup.

Serve the same day as they will go soft by the next day.

Znood el set

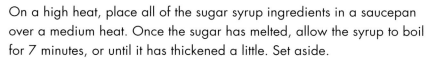

Ladyfinger pastry

1 packet filo pastry
1 lb/500 g ghee, for frying (you can also use canola oil)

RICOTTA MIXTURE
14 oz/400 g ricotta
zest of 1 lemon
1 tablespoon orange blossom water
2 tablespoons superfine/caster sugar

SUGAR SYRUP
1 tablespoon rose water
1 tablespoon orange blossom water
juice of ½ lemon
14 oz/400 g superfine/caster sugar
3 tablespoons water

TOPPING
1 tablespoon lemon zest
2 tablespoons dry roasted pistachios, chopped
few sprigs of mint leaves

Makes 20

On a high heat, place all of the sugar syrup ingredients in a saucepan over a medium heat. Once the sugar has melted, allow the syrup to boil for 7 minutes, or until it has thickened a little. Set aside.

To make the ricotta mixture, mix the ricotta, lemon zest, orange blossom water and sugar together and set aside.

Remove the filo pastry from packet and unroll but keep them layered on top of each other. Separate 6 filo pastry sheets. Place a kitchen towel over the rest to stop it from drying out. Cut the 6 sheets of pastry in half so you have 2 lots of filo, about 2 in/4 cm wide, the same length beside each other.

Place 1 tablespoon of the ricotta at the top of the filo pastry. Fold in the edges of the filo so the sides are closed tightly and no ricotta is able to escape. Roll it up tightly. Repeat with the rest of the filo pastry.

Once you have done as many as you desire, place a tea towel on top of them so they don't dry out.

Heat the ghee in a saucepan on high heat. Once hot, start to fry the pastry, three at a time, but do not overcrowd the pan. Once golden all over, remove the pastries using a slotted spoon and put straight into the sugar syrup. Toss around to coat for about 40 seconds and then remove to a serving plate.

Once you have cooked all of the pastries, sprinkle them with chopped pistachio, a few mint leaves and a pinch of lemon zest.

Note: Traditionally Lebanese pastry would use a clotted cream called ashta in many of our pastry dishes but I have used ricotta here. You could also fill these with Mohalabiya (see recipe p. 112).

Pistachio ice cream

9 oz/250 g unsalted pistachios,
  shelled
15 oz/450 g superfine/caster
  sugar
3 large eggs
17½ fl oz/500 ml milk
1 tablespoon orange blossom water
10 fl oz/290 ml thickened cream

Makes about 1 pt/500 ml

Blend all ingredients, except the cream, in a blender.

Place a saucepan of water on the stove and bring the water to a gentle simmer. This will be a water bath to cook the custard.

Pour the blended ingredients into a bowl, larger than the saucepan. Place the bowl over the top of the saucepan and whisk in the cream. Keep stirring until the mixture coats the back of the spoon.

Allow the mixture to cool down then place it into an ice cream machine and churn it according to the manufacturer's instructions then freeze, giving it a whisk every 20 minutes until it sets.

Coconut chocolate brownies

¾ cup all-purpose/plain flour

¾ cup cocoa powder

½ teaspoon baking powder

2½ oz/70 g milk chocolate buttons

2½ oz/70 g white chocolate
    buttons

¼ cup shredded coconut

2½ oz/80 g roasted walnuts,
    chopped

1¼ cup superfine/caster sugar

6 oz/180 g melted butter

4 eggs, lightly beaten

1 teaspoon orange blossom water
    (if you don't have any use vanilla
    essence)

GANACHE
¼ cup thickened cream

4½ oz/130 g milk chocolate
    buttons

Makes 12

Preheat the oven to 320°F/160°C fan-forced.

Grease and line a rectangular baking tin.

Sift the flour, cocoa powder and baking powder together in a bowl. Add the chocolate buttons, coconut, walnuts and sugar and mix well.

Add the butter and eggs to the flour mixture and mix well to combine. Pour the mixture into the lined baking tin. Bake in the oven for about 40 minutes until slightly firm in the centre. Turn the oven off and leave the brownies to cool down in the oven.

To make the ganache, place a saucepan with water over a medium heat and bring to a boil. Place a heatproof bowl over the saucepan and add in the cream and chocolate. Stir the mixture and let the chocolate melt. Once melted, pour it over the chocolate brownie. Once the ganache has set, cut into the desired size.

Katayef with ashta
Pancakes filled with ashta

3½ cups all-purpose/plain flour
2 tablespoons superfine/caster
    sugar
1 teaspoon baking powder
Pinch of salt
4 cups milk

SUGAR SYRUP
1 tablespoon rose water
1 tablespoon orange blossom water
juice of ½ lemon
14 oz/400 g superfine/caster
    sugar
3 tablespoons water

TOPPING
rose petal jam (can be bought from
    Middle Eastern pastry shops)
finely ground pistachios

1 lb/500 g ashta (can be bought
    from Middle Eastern pastry shops)

Makes about 30

In a large bowl, mix the flour, sugar, baking powder and salt together and whisk in the milk to make a runny pancake batter. Pour through a sieve to make sure there are no lumps. Cover the mixture with a kitchen towel and leave for 2 hours.

Place all the sugar syrup ingredients together in a saucepan over a high heat. Bring to a boil for 7 minutes or until thickened. Once thickened, remove from the heat and set aside.

Place a heavy-based frying pan on a medium heat. Once the pan is hot, pour half a ladle of batter into the pan. Once the pancake is bubbly, throw it away. Do this for the next pancake you make—these are to test that the pan is hot enough. If the batter is too thick add some more milk and give it a good mix.

Continue with the rest of the batter. Once the pancakes are bubbly on top and golden underneath, remove and place on a kitchen towel and leave to cool.

Once cooled, place 1 tablespoon of ashta in the centre of the round pancake. Fold the pancake into a half circle and pinch one end closed, leaving the centre and the other end open. Place all of the pancakes on a platter.

Drizzle the sugar syrup on top of the katayef and sprinkle with pistachio and rose petal jam.

Kanafeh nabelsiyeh

Palestinian kanafeh

2 packets kataifi pastry (see note)
8 tablespoons ghee
2 lb 4 oz/1 kg ashta (see note)

SUGAR SYRUP
1 tablespoon rose water
1 tablespoon orange blossom water
juice of ½ lemon
14 oz/400 g superfine/caster
   sugar
3 tablespoons water

Makes 8

Preheat the oven to 350°F/180°C. You will need 2 baking trays the same size.

In a saucepan over a high heat, bring all the sugar syrup ingredients to a boil. Boil for 7 minutes or until thickened. Set aside.

Spread one packet of the katafi pastry in each tray and flatten with your hands. This will need to be 1 cm in height. Drizzle the melted ghee evenly over each layer of pastry.

Place the trays in the oven and bake for 10–15 minutes until golden brown. Remove from the oven and set aside to cool.

Once the pastry has cooled, spread one of them with the ashta. Carefully place the other pastry on top of the ashta, removing the tray from the top layer, then bake the pastry sandwich for 7 minutes. Remove from the oven and drizzle the syrup all over.

To serve, cut desired shapes out of the pastry and enjoy.

Note: Kataifi pastry resembles vermicelli noodles. It can be purchased from Middle Eastern grocery shops.

If you can't find ashta, you can use 500 g ricotta and 500 g mozarella, shredded, mixed together.

My parents were always cooking food, especially sweets, when I was growing up. They had owned a sweet shop, but it was sold before I was born. By the time I came along it was just my two younger brothers and I still at home, but my parents would still be in the kitchen every day making enough food for guests and relatives who dropped by.

One special occasion was Eid-al Fitr, when we celebrate the end of Ramadan and of fasting, by feasting! After fasting for a month, the last day is the most special. My brothers and I would race home from school to find the kitchen covered in trays and trays of mamoul (see recipe on following page), which my parents would have spent all day making. It would then be our task to decorate each and every biscuit with icing sugar. The biscuits would be offered to guests and relatives over the Eid feast celebration. These were very special occasion biscuits, made only twice a year, and we would not be allowed to eat them until dinner later that evening. But we would always steal some mamoul and run away to eat them. I'm sure our parents saw us but they always acted as though they didn't notice. Although, later, when we refused dinner because we had eating too many stolen biscuits I'm sure they knew exactly why we weren't hungry.

Mamoul

Mahlab is an aromatic spice made from the seeds of a species of cherry, very popular in the Mediterranean (where it is known as 'mahlepi) and the Middle East.

1 lb/500 g fine semolina

1 lb/500 g coarse semolina

2 tablespoons dried yeast

1 tablespoon mahlab (can be bought at a Middle Eastern grocer)

2 tablespoons sugar

1 lb/500 g ghee, melted to room temperature

2 tablespoons rose water

2 tablespoons orange blossom water

1 cup warm milk

FILLING

1 lb/500 g pistachio, unsalted or walnuts, coarsely chopped

½ cup sugar

2 tablespoons rose water

2 tablespoons orange blossom water

TOPPING

2 lb 4 oz/1 kg confectioner's/icing sugar

Makes 22

Preheat the oven to 365°F/185°C. Line a baking tray with baking paper.

In a large bowl, place both types of semolina, yeast, mahlab and sugar and give it a good mix to combine.

Pour in the ghee and mix with your hands until well combined. Add the milk and water and mix to form a dough. Allow to rest for 30 minutes then mix again.

Place all the filling ingredients in a separate bowl.

Roll the dough into balls the size of golf balls. Make a hollow in the centre of a ball and add 1 tablespoon of pistachio mixture in the centre then close the ball up. Repeat with the remaining balls.

Place the finished balls onto a baking tray. Bake for 20 minutes or until golden.

Once the mamoul has cooled down, place the confectioner's sugar through a sieve and sprinkle sugar on top of mamoul until completely covered.

Note: There is a utensil you can use specifically to shape the mamoul. This can be bought from a Middle Easter grocer. Place the ball in the mamoul utensil, flatten the top bit of the dough then flip it over and give it a little tap onto the bench.

Riz be halib
Rice pudding

8½ pints/4 litre full cream milk
½ cup medium grain rice
1 cup superfine/caster sugar
3 tablespoons orange blossom water
1 tablespoon rose water

Makes 16

Place the milk in a heavy-based saucepan and bring to a boil.

Once it has come to the boil, add the rice, bring to a simmer and stir every 10 minutes until the rice becomes very tender (this may take a while). Do not scrape the bottom of the pan as you don't want any burnt milk to come up into the mixture.

Once the rice is tender, add in the sugar, rose water and orange blossom water and give the rice a stir. Keep the pan on the heat until the mixture has thickened.

Once thickened, ladle the mixture into bowls or cups. Cover with cling film that lightly touches the top of the mixture so that no skin forms. Refrigerate and enjoy cold.

Makroum

4 cups all-purpose/plain flour
2 cups fine semolina
2 cups warm canola oil
2 tablespoons baking powder
1 tablespoon ground aniseed
oil for frying

SUGAR SYRUP
1 tablespoon rose water
1 tablespoon orange blossom water
juice of ½ lemon
14 oz/400 g superfine/caster
   sugar
3 tablespoons water

Makes 30

To make the sugar syrup, place all the ingredients into a saucepan over a high heat. Bring to a boil and cook for 7 minutes or until thickened. Remove from heat and set aside until needed.

Mix the remaining ingredients, except the oil, into a bowl and incorporate with your hands to form a dough. Roll out into a log then cut it up into ½ in pieces. Roll the pieces onto the back of a sieve to imprint the crisscross on it.

Place a saucepan on high heat and heat the oil. Deep fry the makrum until golden brown. Remove with a slotted spoon and place in the sugar syrup for a few minutes. Remove and leave to cool before serving.

Hariseh
Coconut slice

1 cup fine semolina
1 cup coarse semolina
1¼ cup superfine/caster sugar
1 cup shredded coconut
½ cup blanched halved almonds
1 cup melted unsalted butter
½ cup warm milk
1 tablespoon rose water
1 tablespoon orange blossom water
2 tablespoons tahini paste

SUGAR SYRUP
1 tablespoon rose water
1 tablespoon orange blossom water
juice of ½ lemon
14 oz/400 g sugar
3 tablespoons water

Makes 25

Place all syrup ingredients into a saucepan and bring to a boil for 7 minutes. Remove from the heat and leave aside to cool.

In a bowl, mix both types of semolina, sugar, coconut, almonds and butter together until well combined and everything is well coated in butter. Slowly add the warm milk, rose water and orange blossom water and mix until it resembles a cake batter mixture but is not too runny.

Cover the base and sides of a square baking dish, around 8 in/20 cm, with tahini paste. Pour the mixture into the dish and give the dish 2 knocks on the bench to get any air bubbles out. Set aside for 4 hours before baking—you will find the top has set a little.

Preheat the oven to 320°F/160°C (or 350°F/180°C fan-forced).

Score the top of the hariseh to form diamond shapes but do not cut all the way through. Place a halved blanched almond in the centre of each diamond.

Bake for 25–30 minutes until dark golden all over. If your dish does not colour evenly then keep rotating the tray in the oven—you need an even colour all over.

Take the tray out and cut the scored line deep to the bottom of the tray. Make sure the sugar syrup is hot then ladle on 1½ cups of the sugar syrup evenly over the hariseh. Add more if needed. The hariseh should absorb all of the sugar syrup.

Allow to rest for 2 hours, or even better over night, before cutting into it and serving. If you don't allow the hariseh to rest it will fall apart.

Sesame snaps

2 cups sesame seeds, toasted to
    golden colour
½ cup honey
½ cup brown sugar

Makes 10

Line a baking tray with baking paper. Place the toasted sesame in a bowl.

Place a saucepan on high heat and add the honey and sugar. Once melted leave on a simmer for a few minutes.

Add 1 tablespoon at a time to the sesame seeds and stir in well to combine.

Pour the sesame mixture onto the tray. Place a piece of baking paper on top and roll out with a rolling pin to make a thin even layer. Take off the baking paper and allow to cool for 10 minutes. Cut into desired size and allow to cool completely before serving.

Umm ali

Egyptian bread pudding

36 fl oz/1 litre milk

21 oz/600 g leftover white bread, no crust

7 oz/200 g superfine/caster sugar

14 oz/400 ml evaporated milk

2 tablespoons blanched almonds

2 tablespoons unsalted pistachios, shelled

3½ oz/100 g raisins

2 teaspoons cinnamon

Makes 4

Preheat the oven to 375°F/190°C.

Pour the milk on top of the bread. Once the bread has soaked up all the milk, place it through a sieve and allow it to drain.

Place bread and sugar into a saucepan on medium–high heat and stir until it has formed a dough-like consistency.

Add the evaporated milk, nuts, raisins and cinnamon to the bread and mix well.

Pour the mixture into a baking dish and bake for 20 minutes or until golden on top.

Thank you

A big thank you to Salt and Pepper for sponsoring me. Also thanks to the Islamic Museum of Australia for giving me the opportunity to open my first café and for allowing me to have the photo shoot in the museum.

Thank you to my mum, who cooked and helped out at the photo shoot.

To my husband and children for making me realise that dreams do come true and for helping me to hold on. You taught me to not give up and that life is too short. Without Mahmoud El Khafir my husband pushing and encouraging me I would never have made it to the top three on MasterChef.

I just want to thank all of my family so much for their support and love. A special thanks to my manager/brother Mahamoud Fahour for his support and determination to help me build a brand and a company. He is also an amazing brother.

Index

First published in 2014 by New Holland Publishers Pty Ltd
London • Sydney • Cape Town • Auckland

The Chandlery Unit 114 50 Westminster Bridge Road London SE1 7QY United Kingdom
1/66 Gibbes Street Chatswood NSW 2067 Australia
Estuaries No 4 Oxbow Crescent, Century Avenue, Century City 7441 South Africa
218 Lake Road Northcote Auckland New Zealand

www.newhollandpublishers.com

A record of this book is held at the British Library and the National Library of Australia.

ISBN 9781742575360

Managing Director: Fiona Schultz
Publisher: Diane Ward
Project Editor: Jodi De Vantier
Designer: Lorena Susak
Photographs: Greg Elms
Food stylist: Georgia Young
Proofreader: Tricia Cortese
Production Director: Olga Dementiev
Printer: Toppan Leefung Printing Ltd., China

10 9 8 7 6 5 4 3 2 1

Our thanks to the Islamic Museum of Australia and Salt and Pepper.

Keep up with New Holland Publishers on Facebook
www.facebook.com/NewHollandPublishers